How to Draw
HORSES
and Ponies

Peter Gray

PowerKiDS
press.

Published in 2014 by The Rosen Publishing Group, Inc.
29 East 21st Street, New York, NY 10010

Illustrations: © Peter Gray
Editors: Joe Harris and Nicola Barber
U.S. Editor: Joshua Shadowens
Design: sprout.uk.com
Cover design: sprout.uk.com

Library of Congress Cataloging-in-Publication Data

Gray, Peter, 1969–
 How to draw horses and ponies / by Peter Gray.
    pages cm. — (How to draw animals)
 Includes index.
 ISBN 978-1-4777-1303-7 (library binding) — ISBN 978-1-4777-1417-1 (pbk.) — ISBN 978-1-4777-1418-8 (6-pack)
 1. Horses in art. 2. Drawing—Technique. I. Title.
 NC783.8.H65G74 2014
 743.6'96655—dc23
                    2012047581

Printed in China

SL002689US

CPSIA Compliance Information: Batch #AS3102PK: For Further Information contact Rosen Publishing, New York, New York at 1-800-237-9932

CONTENTS

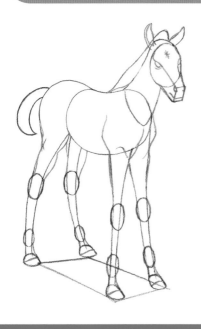

DRAWING

You should start your drawings with simple guidelines before fleshing them out with detail.

Build up the general shape of your subject with guidelines. I have drawn the guidelines heavily to make them easy to follow, but you should work faintly with a hard pencil.

Guidelines

Use a softer pencil to develop the character and details. You may find that you do not follow the guidelines exactly in places. That's fine—they are only a rough guide.

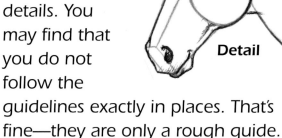

Detail

Carefully erase the guidelines and mistakes. Then add shading and **texture** with a soft pencil.

Shading and texture

INKING

For a bold look, go over the outlines with ink. Wait for the ink to dry thoroughly, then erase all the pencil marks.

The easiest inking method is to use a felt-tip pen. If you plan to add paint at a later stage, make sure your pen is waterproof.

Felt-tip pen outlines

For a more graceful effect, use a fine-tipped watercolor brush dipped in ink.

Brush outlines

COLORING

Although I use watercolors in this book, the main principles are the same for any materials—start with the shading, then add in markings and textures, and finally, work your main colors over the top.

Felt-tip coloring

Felt-tip pens produce bright, vibrant colors. Work quickly so that the pen strokes do not remain visible.

Colored pencils

Colored pencils are the easiest coloring tools to use, but you have to take great care to blend the colors to achieve a good finish.

Watercolors

The subtlest effects can be achieved with watercolor paints. It is best to buy them as a set of solid blocks that you wet with a brush. Mix the colors in a palette or on an old white plate.

HEAD SHAPE

The horse has a long and narrow head. Here are some tips for getting its shape right.

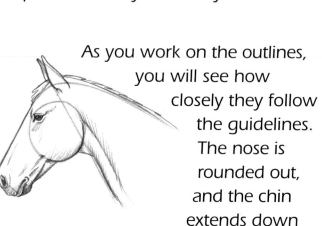

These are the basic guidelines for a horse's head. The nose is long and straight, and the neck is broad. Draw a circle for the cheek. This circle will help you to position the eye correctly.

As you work on the outlines, you will see how closely they follow the guidelines. The nose is rounded out, and the chin extends down a little. The eye, ear, and mane will need some more detail.

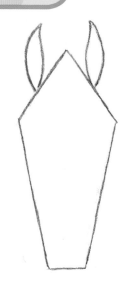

A front view shows you the width of the animal's head between its eyes. The lower part of the head is much narrower.

A good way to get the nostrils right is to think of the left one as a number "6" and the right one as its mirror image. Note how close together the ears sit at the top of the head.

Dished face

Roman nose

VARIATIONS
The basic face shape varies in different breeds of horses and ponies. Noses may be longer or shorter. Heads may be thinner or broader.

These are two quite extreme versions, one with a "dished" face (an upturned nose) and the other with a downturned or "Roman" nose.

BODY SHAPE

Here we look at the horse's body structure in three different ways.

This diagram shows the way that a horse's body can be measured in head lengths. An average horse is about three head lengths tall at the shoulder. Its torso (main body) is also three head lengths long. However, these **proportions** can be different for horses of different breeds and ages.

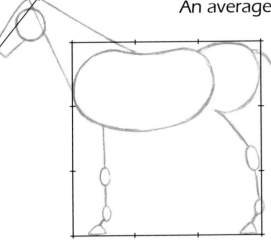

Proportions

Front view

This skeleton view of a horse should help you to make sense of the joints. The shoulder bones push forward from the chest and the hips angle backward. Notice where the joints are found in the legs.

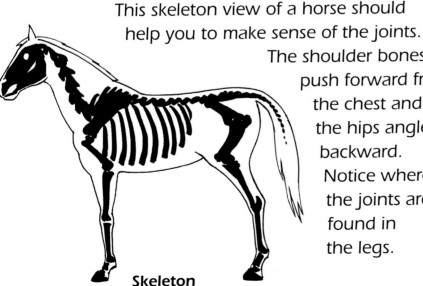

Skeleton

Viewed from the front, you can see that the shoulders are narrow, the hips wider, and the belly rounded and broad. Note how close together the legs are on the ground.

THOROUGHBRED

A thoroughbred is a breed of horse used for racing, jumping, and other **equestrian** sports. Thoroughbreds are usually agile, quick, and lively.

1 Begin by drawing a large oval with a flat top. This is the main part of the horse's chest and belly. Add a small circle for the head and a long curve off the animal's rear end for its rump. Leave enough space on the paper for the legs and tail.

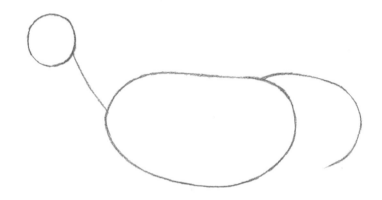

2 Draw the cone shape of the **muzzle** and then add a line for the back of the neck, arching over the head. Sketch in the long, thin curves of the legs, which become narrower toward the feet.

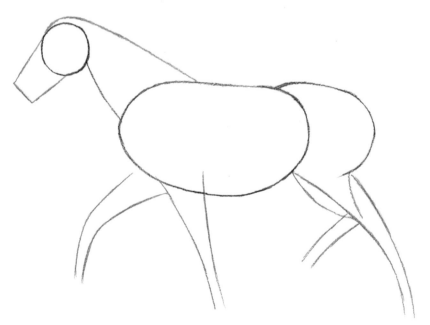

3 Horses' legs have visible joints, which look very knobbly. It's a good idea to draw fairly large ovals on the legs for each joint, taking care to place them correctly. Sketch the mane and tail as simple shapes without texture or detail.

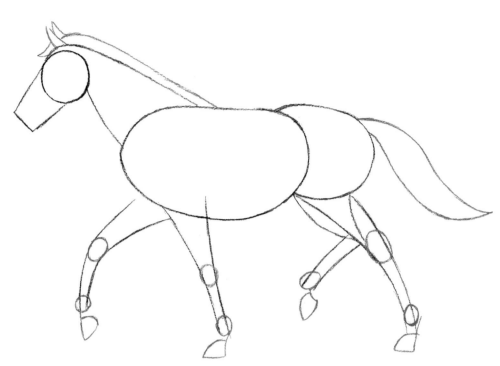

4 Now that the guidelines are finished, you can start on the details. Draw the main features of the face and the shape of the harness. Work on the upper legs. Note the bulky shoulder area at the front of the chest above the leading (front) leg.

5 Work on the detail using a sharp pencil and an eraser. Make the body curves smooth and graceful, and pay attention to the muscles and joints of the legs. Work on the head and harness, then add some flowing texture to the mane and tail.

6 When you are happy with your outlines, it's time to ink them in. Use fine, confident strokes. Move the paper around on your desk to allow your arm to work freely. When the ink is dry, all the pencil work can be erased to leave a clean outline.

7 You can break the coloring process down into stages. For this horse, I decided to start with the dark markings. I mixed dark brown and blue to make black. Where the markings blend into the upper leg, I used a dampened brush to soften the hard edge of the paint marks. I also added some shading to the ankles and hooves.

FAMOUS HORSES

Thoroughbreds are ridden by people in a wide range of sporting events. Many are trained to be racers—either on flat courses with no jumps or in races with fences and ditches. The most successful of these horses have become racing legends, with names such as Man o' War, Kelso, and Native Dancer.

ANIMAL FACTS

8 To add shading to the body, I mixed up a warm dark brown color. I used this color for the darkest areas under the belly and inside the legs. Where the shading was less dark, I watered down the paint. Then I softened the edges of the painted areas with a wet brush and clean tissue paper.

9 Once the shading is complete, wash the main color on in broad strokes. Keep the paint flowing and do not allow any hard edges to become dry as you work. When the area is covered, leave it to dry completely.

10 When the paint is dry, you can add other small areas of color and strengthen the shading. Then work on the sheen to make the horse look glossy. I wet the areas of **highlight** with a brush, then dabbed off the moistened paint with a clean tissue. You might prefer to create highlights with watered-down white ink or chalk. Add a few spots of white ink to bring out the highlights on the head.

FOAL

A foal is a baby horse, up to one year old. Foals have very long legs and small, slim bodies. Their manes and tails are short. After its first birthday, a foal is known as a yearling.

1 Although a foal is much leaner than a fully-grown horse, you start with a similar oval for the chest and belly. Add a circle for the head and a long curve off the animal's rear end for its rump.

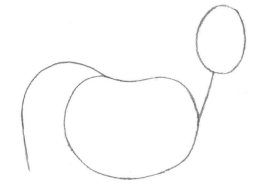

2 Draw in the muzzle and the neck, arching over the head. Sketch in the legs, which are very long and thin in a foal.

LONG LEGS

When a foal is born, its legs are almost as long as they will be when it has grown into an adult horse. Unlike human babies, foals use their legs almost right away. A foal will be standing within an hour of birth, and by one day old, it will be trotting and galloping next to its mother.

ANIMAL FACTS

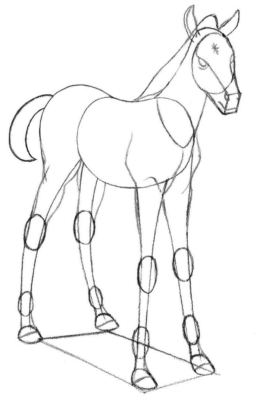

3 Draw the head as a roughly rectangular box at this stage. The knees are very knobbly, and the tail and mane are short. To place the legs firmly on the ground, draw a neat shape on the floor to guide you.

4 Now draw in the main features of the face and the ears. Work on the upper legs, bringing out the curves of the foal's muscles. Add some detail to the hooves.

5 Continue working on the detail of the head, mane, and short tail. Make the body curves smooth, and pay attention to the joints on the foal's long legs.

6 To give a softer feel for this young animal, I decided on colored ink for part of the outline. I used a yellow-brown color for the body and upper legs and black ink for the darker parts.

7 Although the nose is as dark as the legs and tail, it is more gray in color. A young horse is not as sleek and shiny as an adult. To give a sense of the fluffier coat, I painted some short, soft strokes on the foal's body.

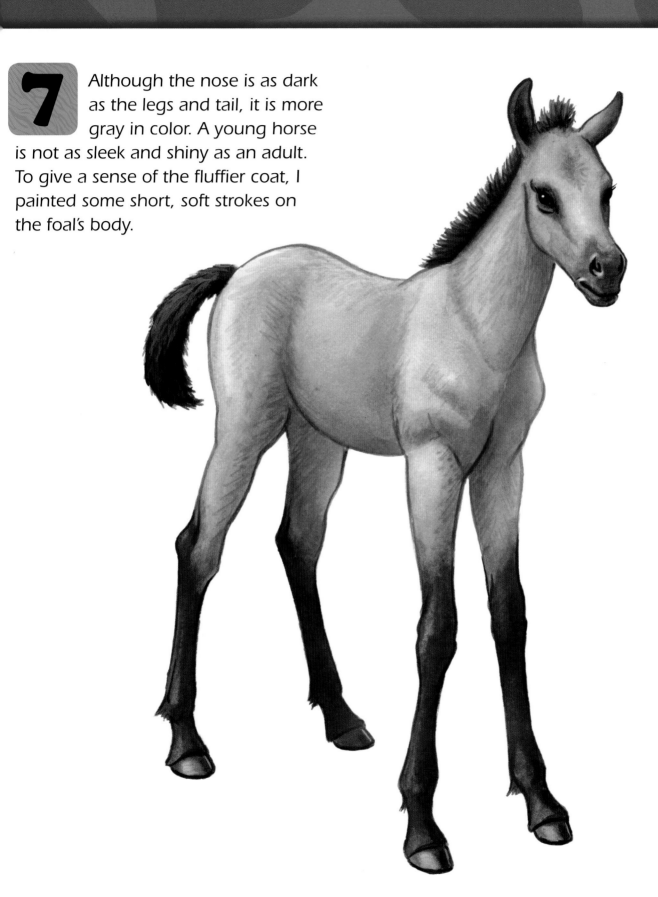

WILD HORSE

Most of the wild horses around the world are related to **domesticated** animals that escaped or strayed. These horses have gone back to the wild, where they usually live in small groups.

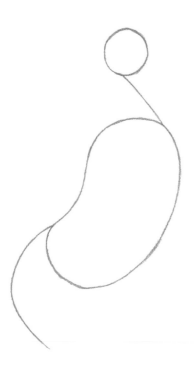

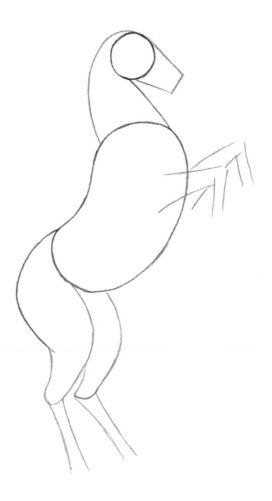

1 This wild horse is up on its hind legs, so position the large oval of the body at an angle. The head circle sits on top, and the line of the animal's rear end curves in below.

2 Draw the cone shape of the muzzle, then add the line for the back of the neck, arching over the head. Add the angles of the two front legs. The powerful back legs reach down to the ground.

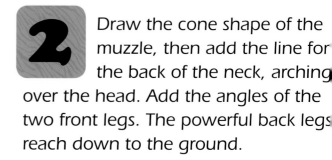

7 When I had colored and shaded the animal, I added lots of fine strokes to capture the texture of the coat. This pony's rough coat has little natural sheen, so I kept the highlights to a minimum on the body. I used white ink for the mane and tail and the shaggy legs.

A PRAIRIE SCENE

Now it's time to test your skills by putting some of the horses in this book into a suitable scene. You can choose any of the different kinds of horses we have drawn.

1 When you are creating a scene, it is a good idea to start with a rough version of your artwork. I decided to set two wild ponies against a background scene of windswept prairies. I created a rough drawing and figured out a shading scheme, with the light coming from the right-hand side and a dark, stormy sky.

2 To figure out a rough color scheme, quickly apply some color to your pencil rough. I chose to use the colors of fall—yellows, greens, and browns, with a heavy purple-gray sky.

3 When the paint is dry, develop your color rough with some dark outlining. I decided to make the distant pony dark in color to stand out against its pale background. I also darkened the sky and some of the shadows, then Iw added a few bright highlights with white ink.

4 On a large sheet of good paper, draw the guidelines for your final picture. Apart from the ponies, there was not much detailed drawing required for my scene, but I sketched in the general forms of the landscape.

5 Work some more pencil detail into the scene, including all the marks you will need for inking. I completed the drawings of the ponies and worked on the general textures of the landscape. Instead of drawing every stone in the wall, I made marks to guide my inking brush.

6 Now it's time for inking. I inked in the trees over the rough pencil marks, as well as the wall and the grass, all rather loosely. I was more careful with the ponies. Then I marked in the distant horizon with a few swift strokes of thinly diluted ink.

7 Before starting on the color, I worked on the dark areas of the picture. I mixed two shades of dark gray out of blue, dark red, and brown. Then I painted them over the sky area with a large brush. I used the same color for the darker areas of shading on the animals.

8 For the color, I mixed up several grass colors using greens, browns, and yellows. I painted them quickly over the grass, to create a feel of rough, scrubby grassland. I darkened the sky and the horse's shadows a little more. Then I worked up the **foreground**, using more inks, both black and white, to strengthen and develop the various textures.

31

GLOSSARY

domesticated (duh-MES-tih-kayt-ed) Describes an animal that has been tamed and adapted by humans to work for them.

equestrian (ih-KWES-tree-un) Relating to or involving horses.

foreground (for-GROWND) The front part of a picture.

highlight (HY-lyt) A bright area in a painting or drawing.

muzzle (MUH-zel) The nose and mouth of an animal.

proportions (pruh-POR-shunz) Relating the size of one thing to another.

texture (TEKS-chur) The feel of a surface.

WEBSITES

Due to the changing nature of Internet links, PowerKids Press has developed an online list of websites related to the subject of this book. This site is updated regularly. Please use this link to access the list:

www.powerkidslinks.com/HTDA/hors

FURTHER READING

Ames, Lee J. *Draw 50 Animals.* New York: Watson-Guptill, 2012.

Hart, Christopher. *Young Artists Draw Animals.* New York: Watson-Guptill, 2012.

Ransford, Sandy. *The Kingfisher Illustrated Horse and Pony Encyclopedia.* London, England: Kingfisher PLC, 2010.

INDEX